My Personal Data Keeper

Table of Contents

Introduction

The Basics

Medication

Educational/Military History

Notes

Family and Friends

Household Pets

Insurance Information

Financial Information

Legal Documents

Final Arrangements

Log-Ins and Passwords

Important Phone Numbers

Miscellaneous Notes

Introduction

Congratulations on the purchase of your Personal Data Keeper (PDK)!

Most of us can recite our Social Security Numbers and the Phone Numbers of close family and friends when we feel healthy and alert. However, during a medical emergency, accident or household trauma, those things we save to memory may not come to mind so easily and when asked we may not be able to remember the phone numbers of our closest relatives or where to locate that information.

For that simple reason, I have created this book that will help you compile a picture of your life to put your most important information at your fingertips and for those who may need to access it in the event of an emergency.

Who will use this PDK?

- Individuals who travel frequently
- Individuals with medical conditions
- Someone who lives alone
- Everyone

How should you use this PDK?

- Keep close at hand for quick reference
- Pack it in your luggage when you travel
- Give a copy to your adult children or POA
- Keep a copy with your Legal Documents

Let us start at the beginning with who you are. Basic identifying information that provides those who may be trying to assist you with pertinent knowledge of where to begin searching for answers and more assistance.

The Basics

Full Name	
Date of Birth	
Place of Birth	
Religion	
Marital Status	
Name of S/O	
Driver License Number	
Social Security Number	
Father's Name	
Father's Place of Birth	
Mother's Name	
Mother's Place of Birth	

Medication

List all currents medications. You will want to review this list frequently and maintain the most current information by updating this information when changes in medication or dosages occur.

Date: _____ Prescription: _____

Dosage: _____ Taken for: _____

Date: _____ Prescription: _____

Dosage: _____ Taken for: _____

Date: _____ Prescription: _____

Dosage: _____ Taken for: _____

Date: _____ Prescription: _____

Dosage: _____ Taken for: _____

Date: _____ Prescription: _____

Dosage: _____ Taken for: _____

Date: _____ Prescription: _____

Dosage: _____ Taken for: _____

Educational and Military History

Educational and Military information is important because it is a part of who you are. List Military service and schools and college attended even if you did not reach graduation. This is information that is often not passed onto family members and can be sometimes forgotten.

Military Branch: _____

Rank: _____

High School: _____

Graduation Year: _____

College/Trade School: _____

Graduation Year: _____

College/Trade School: _____

Graduation Year: _____

College/Trade School: _____

Graduation Year: _____

Notes:

_____

_____

_____

_____

_____

_____

_____

_____

_____

_____

_____

_____

_____

_____

_____

_____

_____

_____

_____

_____

Family and Friends

List family members and friends who should be contacted in the event of a medical or household emergency. Example: Immediate neighbors, adult children, Power of Attorney, etc.

Name: _____

Address: _____

Phone: _____Relationship: _____

Name: _____

Address: _____

Phone: _____Relationship: _____

Name: _____

Address: _____

Phone: _____Relationship: _____

Name: _____

Address: _____

Phone: _____Relationship: _____

Family and Friends

Name: _____

Address: _____

Phone: _____Relationship: _____

Name: _____

Address: _____

Phone: _____Relationship: _____

Name: _____

Address: _____

Phone: _____Relationship: _____

Name: _____

Address: _____

Phone: _____Relationship: _____

Name: _____

Address: _____

Phone: _____Relationship: _____

Household Pets

Pets quickly become family and a major part of our lives and it is important to remember they depend on us for their basic daily needs of food and shelter. When we aren't available or able, no one may be there to give them the care they have been depending on.

The first step in providing for the pets you love is to understand the possibility that at some point, someone else may need to tend to their daily needs. Then consider that not everyone may be the right someone for your pet.

Be selective and assign a designated person who is not only able but who has also agreed to be contacted in the event of an emergency.

———————————

Pet Name: _____

Pet Name: _____

Pet Name: _____

Veterinarian: _____

Phone: _____

Designated contact regarding care of pets in an emergency (name, address and phone number):

_____

_____

_____

Additional Notes:

_____

_____

_____

_____

_____

_____

_____

Insurance Information

Health Insurance:

Insurance Company: _____

Policy Number: _____

Address: _____

_____Phone: _____

Auto Insurance:

Insurance Company: _____

Policy Number: _____

Address: _____

_____Phone: _____

Home Owner's/Renter's Insurance:

Insurance Company: _____

Policy Number: _____

Address: _____

_____Phone: _____

Life Insurance:

Insurance Company: _____

Policy Number: _____

Address: _____

_____Phone: _____

Insurance Company: _____

Policy Number: _____

Address: _____

_____Phone: _____

Insurance Company: _____

Policy Number: _____

Address: _____

_____Phone: _____

Bank Information

Bank Name: _____

Address: _____

Phone: _____

Account Number: _____Type: _____

Bank Name: _____

Address: _____

Phone: _____

Account Number: _____Type: _____

Bank Name: _____

Address: _____

Phone: _____

Account Number: _____Type: _____

Bank Name: _____

Address: _____

Phone: _____

Account Number: _____Type: _____

Credit Cards

Company Name: _____

Phone: _____

Account Number: _____

Company Name: _____

Phone: _____

Account Number: _____

Company Name: _____

Phone: _____

Account Number: _____

Company Name: _____

Phone: _____

Account Number: _____

Company Name: _____

Phone: _____

Account Number: _____

Legal Documents

Power of Attorney Name: _____

Location of Document: _____

WILL: _____

Location of Document: _____

Advance Directives: _____

Location of Document: _____

Birth Certificate: _____

Location of Document: _____

Marriage License: _____

Location of Document: _____

Divorce Papers: _____

Location of Document: _____

Vehicle Titles: _____

Location of Document(s): _____

Property Deed: _____

Location of Document: _____

Final Arrangements

Church: _____

Address: _____

Phone: _____

Funeral Home: _____

Address: _____

Phone: _____

Cemetery: _____

Address: _____

Phone: _____

Log-Ins and Passwords

List Item	Log-In	Password	PIN

Important Phone Numbers

Physician Name: _____

Address: _____

Phone: _____

Physician Name: _____

Address: _____

Phone: _____

Physician Name: _____

Address: _____

Phone: _____

Attorney Name: _____

Address: _____

Phone: _____

Pastor Name: _____

Address: _____

Phone: _____

Miscellaneous Notes

_____

_____

_____

_____

_____

_____

_____

_____

_____

_____

_____

_____

_____

_____

_____

_____

_____

_____